Fanny Crosby

Queen of Gospel Songs

Books by Rebecca Davis

With Daring Faith

Fanny Crosby: Queen of Gospel Songs

Rebecca Davis

Fanny Crosby
Queen of Gospel Songs

JOURNEY FORTH™

Greenville, South Carolina

Library of Congress Cataloging-in-Publication Data

Davis, Rebecca Henry.
    Fanny Crosby : queen of gospel songs / by Rebecca Davis.
    p. cm.
Summary: A biography of the nineteenth-century blind woman who
wrote more than 9,000 hymns.
    ISBN 1-57924-970-1 (alk. paper)
    1. Crosby, Fanny, 1820-1915—Juvenile literature. 2. Hymn writ-
ers—United States—Biography—Juvenile literature. 3. Poets, American—19th century—Biography—Juvenile literature. 4. Blind—United
States—Biography—Juvenile literature. 5. Gospel music—History and
criticism—Juvenile literature. [1. Crosby, Fanny, 1820-1915. 2. Hymn
writers. 3. Poets, American. 4. Blind. 5. People with disabilities. 6.
Women—Biography.] I. Title.
    PS3114.V43Z64 2003
    811.4—dc21

                                                          2003008166

Fanny Crosby: Queen of Gospel Songs

Designed by Erin Byram
Cover and illustrations by Kyle Henry

© 2003 BJU Press
Greenville, SC 29614

ISBN 1-57924-970-1

15   14   13   12   11   10   9   8   7   6   5   4   3   2   1

To the memory of my grandparents,
Thomas Marvin Groome and
Minnie Mae Osborne Groome,
who loved Fanny Crosby's hymns

Contents

1 "Something's Wrong with Her Eyes"

"Mother," called Mercy Crosby. "Come look at little baby Fanny. Do you think there's something wrong with her eyes?"

Mercy's mother came in from the kitchen. She studied the tiny baby in Mercy's arms. "They do look peculiar, Mercy," she admitted. "Red and weepy. It's not right." She reached out to take the baby in her own strong arms. "There, there, little Fanny," she whispered. "We'll trust the Lord to take care of these eyes."

Mercy didn't look like much more than a girl herself, but she was Fanny's mama. She and her husband lived with Mercy's parents and their family. In New York in 1820, that's what many families did.

The days passed. Mercy and her mother could tell that the tiny baby definitely had an infection in her eyes. Fanny cried so much that her crying kept the family awake at night.

"I don't know what to do for her!" Mercy said wearily. "The doctor has been away so long!"

"Yes," said Theda, Mercy's fifteen-year-old sister. "And there's no way to know when he's coming back."

John Crosby, Mercy's husband, said, "I heard today that there is a man staying with the Hopkins family. I think he said he was a doctor. Perhaps he can help."

"Oh, please," said Mercy. "Find him, and get some help."

"I'll go!" said Mercy's brother, nine-year-old Joseph. "I can run over there fast. It's only four miles or so."

"Well, you just wait till morning, son," said Joseph's father. "If you go now, it will be dark before you get back."

So, early in the morning, Joseph headed out. When he returned, he was on a horse behind a stranger. "Are you a doctor, sir?" Mercy asked doubtfully.

"Yes, I am," replied the stranger. "I've had much success over in Greene County. I can help all kinds of infections. I use a special mustard plaster." He pulled different mysterious bottles and tools out of his big black bag.

Mercy held Fanny a little closer. "A mustard plaster, sir?" Mercy asked. "Won't that hurt her eyes?"

The stranger chuckled. "Now, now," he said. "You just leave it to me." He mixed things from several dark bottles. Then he held up an awful-smelling, brownish glop.

"Now," said the stranger, "let me see that baby." He reached out for little Fanny. Her eyes looked red and crusted, even when they were closed. "I'll just smear some of this on each eye . . ." As he did so, the tiny baby jumped. Then she began to scream.

The stranger had to shout over Fanny's cries. "This will draw out the infection," he told Mercy. Quickly he gathered his equipment and began to pack his bags.

Mercy's thin face was white with fright. "Are you sure it won't hurt her?"

"It will be fine, just fine." The stranger picked up his hat. "You just wait and see."

"How long should we leave it on?" Mercy shouted.

"Wipe it off in the morning." The man picked up his bag and was out the door.

Late that night Mercy's mother returned from helping a sick woman. When she got inside, she told Mercy, "I could hear Fanny's screams from far down the road."

"Oh, Mother!" Mercy cried. "We're all just sick with worry." Mercy's face was red from weeping. She told her mama the story of the visiting "doctor."

Mercy saw her mother's lips set in a grim line as she went to get a cloth without a word. Then Mercy watched her gently wipe Fanny's eyes. Under her breath she muttered things that Mercy couldn't quite hear.

2 Hard Times

Time passed. Little Fanny's eye infection finally began to clear up. Fanny stopped crying all the time and became more cheerful. She began to do some of the things little babies do. She turned toward the sound of her mother's voice. She held her head up on her own. She began to make soft cooing noises.

But there was still something wrong with Fanny's eyes. The mustard plaster seemed to have hurt them in some way. Her eyes looked almost all white, even where the blue part should have been.

Each Sunday after church meeting, ladies and men would cluster around to see if the scars over Fanny's eyes were still there. They were. "Looks to me like that so-called doctor did her no good," said one woman, unlacing her shoes to carry them home. "No good at all."

The other neighbors were also taking off their shoes. Shoes were never worn in the summertime, except inside the church building. "We ought to find that fellow," said one man. "We ought to let him know what we think of a fellow who would do such a thing to an innocent little baby."

"Mr. Hopkins said he's gone back to Greene County," said another. "That's a long way from Putnam County. I don't even know where it is."

Back at home, Mercy and John waved their hands in front of Fanny's eyes. But her eyes still just stared straight ahead. "She's completely blind," Mercy moaned. She put her hands to her own thin face. "She can't see at all."

"If it is the will of God," said John, "we will just have to make the best of it."

"Perhaps we can find a real doctor," offered Mercy's mother. "Perhaps he could undo the damage that . . . that man did to our little girl."

"It would cost a great sum of money," said John. "We have a hard time making ends meet as it is."

But times were to become even harder for the Crosbys. That fall, before Fanny was even a year old, her father got very sick. A few days later John

Crosby died. Mercy Crosby was a widow now; she was only twenty-one years old.

Soon after her husband was buried, Mercy put on her best dress. The family was so terribly poor that she had to start working for rich people down the road. Now she would be leaving little Fanny all day, every day, except Sunday.

"Goodbye, Mother," Mercy said, without a smile. "You will care well for Fanny, I know." She finished buttoning the thirty-five buttons down the front of her dress. She straightened her stiff white collar.

"I certainly will, my dear," answered her mother with a warm kiss. "Theda and I will keep things going here. Fanny will have a wonderful time with little Polly."

Polly was Mercy's youngest sister. She was only three years old. Mercy could see that Polly thought of her little niece Fanny as if she were a little sister.

Time passed. Each day after Mercy left for work, she knew that her mother and sister would be working hard in the house. They would stoke the fire, prepare the little bit of food, and clean and scrub. They would make the candles, tend the animals, wash or starch or iron the clothes, and care for the two little girls.

In the evening Mercy would return from her servant work for the rich family. Her father and brother would come in from their work in the fields or the barn. Each hungry mouth would receive a bit of bread and beans or potato. Then the family gathered together around the fireplace. Mercy's father went to the small bookshelf and pulled out one of their few books to read to the family. He pushed his long black beard out of the way and settled the large black book in his lap.

Tonight he was reading from *Pilgrim's Progress*. "So Christian went on, and Apollyon met him," he read. "Now the monster was hideous to behold."

The ladies mended shirts and darned socks. Joseph carved a bit of wood. Polly and Fanny quietly played with their cornhusk dolls. All the family listened. As time passed, Fanny began to be able to make pictures in her mind.

3 Nature Walks

"I have been doing some thinking, my dear little Fanny." Fanny's grandma lifted her two-year-old granddaughter up to her lap. "Since you cannot see, I will be your eyes for you. Does that sound like a good plan?"

"Yes, Grandma." Fanny smiled just from the sound in her grandma's voice. She didn't understand what Grandma was talking about. But it didn't matter. She reached up to feel Grandma's eyes and nose and smiling mouth. It was one of the faces that she loved best.

"I'll help, Mother!" cried little Polly, now almost five. "I already show Fanny things outside sometimes. She learns fast!"

"I'll help too, Mother." Theda looked in from her sweeping. "When I have time."

"You do such a good job of the housework for me, Theda. I think now I may have more time to teach Fanny about God's wonderful world. She does learn fast, as you say, Polly. She cannot see, but there is still much we can teach her. We don't want Fanny to be a poor, helpless woman, now do we?" She slid Fanny off her lap and took her hand. "Come," she said. "We're going for a walk." Grandma, Fanny, and Polly walked outside the little house.

May in New York was the time of blooming flowers and singing birds. Grandma and the little girls could practically smell the springtime. "Do you hear the birds, Fanny?" asked Grandma.

"Yes, Grandma," answered Fanny. Polly had already told her that those noises were birds.

"Fanny, our dear Lord Jesus made so many, many different kinds of birds. Every one of them has a certain kind of song. We'll listen closely, and maybe we can hear some. Oh! Did you hear that one? That one that said 'Wonk! Wonk!' "

"Yes!" cried little Fanny.

"That's a big black raven. Why, he's almost as big as you are!"

Fanny clapped her little hands in delight. "A raven!" she cried.

"Ravens brought the prophet Elijah food," Grandma said. "Do you remember our Bible stories? That was when there was no food in the land. That's how God provided for him."

Grandma often walked with Fanny outdoors in the woods. Fanny felt the hard, tough skin on Grandma's fingers as she held her hand. Fanny loved to listen to Grandma's calm, quiet voice as she talked about the birds.

Soon Fanny knew almost every bird in the area by its song. She could even remember how big it was and what color its feathers were.

Grandma taught Fanny about birds and flowers and insects and trees. Fanny never grew tired of learning about the wonders of God's creation.

One beautiful summer morning when Fanny was four, she walked between Grandma and Polly. She held both of their hands tightly in her own.

"I hear the mourning dove, Grandma!" cried Fanny. "It says 'coo-coo.' "

Polly laughed. "I used to think it was called a morning dove, because it came out in the morning. But then I found out it was just supposed to sound sad."

"It does sound sad," Fanny agreed. "Why does it sound sad, Grandma?"

"Well," answered Grandma, "the Lord made it that way. Maybe it was to remind us that we need to be sorry for our sins and turn to Him for salvation. David said that he wanted to fly away like a dove to find rest. But we find our rest in Jesus."

"Noah sent a dove out from the ark!" cried Fanny. "I remember that one too, Grandma!"

That evening Fanny sat with Polly and Grandma on the porch. They were waiting for Fanny's mother to return home from work. Grandma sat in the rocking chair on the porch with Fanny on her lap and Polly at her knee. "The sun is going down behind the hills, Fanny," Grandma said gently.

Fanny snuggled close to Grandma. She patted the familiar bun of hair pulled tight at Grandma's neck.

"I can tell it's going," she said. "The brightness isn't as bright."

"Yes, I'm so glad the Lord allowed you to see light," answered Grandma. "You can get a little idea of the light of the sun. But when the Lord sends the sun down, He does it in a blaze of glory. This evening it's shining red and yellow and pink. And isn't that a little bit of purple there, Polly?" She pointed beyond the spruce tree.

"Yes, I see it, Mother," said Polly. "But it's fading away."

Fanny reached her hand out. "I want to see it too."

"But Fanny, don't you know," said Grandma, patting Fanny's hand, "you can see it through our eyes. We'll tell you about it. You can make up pictures of it in your head."

"What does purple look like, Grandma?" Fanny asked.

Grandma reached down and picked a violet that was growing next to the porch. "Feel this little flower, Fanny," she said. "It's called a violet. Violet is another name for purple. That's what purple looks like."

Fanny felt the flower. "It feels soft," she said. She held it up to the light. "I can see the colors a little bit."

"Yes, I'm so glad you can see color a little," murmured Grandma. "Violets are one of my favorite flowers."

"Where are they growing, Grandma?" Fanny slid down from Grandma's lap and held her hand. They walked carefully down the porch steps so Grandma could show Fanny where the violets grew. Grandma showed Fanny how to follow the stem all the way to the ground to pick it. Fanny picked a whole bouquet. "They're my favorite flower!" she exclaimed. "I love purple!"

"The Lord God made so many different flowers, Fanny," said Grandma. "You can learn about them through your fingers."

Through the spring and summer Grandma showed Fanny one flower after another. She helped Fanny recognize them by their scent and their shape.

"This is called a day lily, Fanny," she explained one afternoon in June. "It blooms for only one day. This might have been the flower Jesus was talking about when he said that the lilies bloom for just a day. But even King Solomon wasn't dressed as gloriously as they are."

"Was King Solomon very rich?" Fanny asked.

"Oh, wonderfully rich," said Grandma. "But Jesus was showing how wonderful are the works of God."

"Mama!" cried Polly. "Here's a little bird on the ground!"

Grandma took Fanny's hand and hurried to the spot. A tiny wren lay dead beside the low stone wall. "How did it die, Mama?" Polly asked anxiously.

"I don't know, dearie. But the Lord knows. Not one bird falls to the ground without His knowing. Our Lord knows everything."

Fanny felt for a stick and used it to carefully stroke the soft feathers. "Poor little bird," she said.

4 God's World and God's Word

In the early fall most of the flowers were gone. Then Fanny walked with Grandma and learned to recognize trees by their bark and leaves.

"Can you imagine, Fanny," Grandma said as they walked, "the dear Lord Jesus made so many different kinds of trees, just as He made so many different kinds of birds. Come here and feel the bark on this one."

"It feels like it's peeling off," said Fanny.

"Yes, you're right," agreed Grandma. "Doesn't it feel a little like paper? That's why we call it a paper birch. Here, feel one of the leaves. Feel it right there, along the edge."

"It's a little bit pokey, like Grandpa's saw!" said Fanny.

"Yes." Grandma chuckled. "Every tree has different bark. Every tree has different kinds of leaves.

Let's see how many we can learn about before the first snow comes."

Before the first snow came, Fanny could identify almost every tree growing around the house. She could tell them by the bark and the shape of the leaves. "Why did the Lord make so many different kinds of trees, Grandma?" she asked.

"Oh, He had lots of different reasons, dearie," answered Grandma. "Different kinds of wood are useful for different things. Different trees give us different kinds of fruits. But mainly I think it was just to show us what a great and mighty God He is. Just think, He made them all when He said, 'Let the earth bring forth grass, the herb yielding seed, and the fruit tree yielding fruit after his kind.' That means that every little seed grows up to be the same kind of tree as its mama tree, you know."

"God can do anything, can't He, Grandma?" said Fanny.

"Oh my, yes," answered Grandma. "He certainly can."

Soon the days grew colder, and the nights came sooner. Grandma and her girls spent more time inside. This was when she read the Bible to them. When Theda had time, she often joined Polly and Fanny for her mother's Bible stories.

One winter afternoon Grandma gathered the girls on the floor around her. Then she sat down in her rocking chair and opened the huge, old Bible.

"Today," Grandma began, "our story comes from the Gospel of John, chapter nine. It's the story of Jesus giving sight to the blind man. It says, 'And as Jesus passed by, he saw a man which was blind from his birth.' "

"I wasn't blind from birth, was I, Grandma?" asked Fanny.

"No, no, you weren't, dearie, but it was soon after." Grandma's lips became set in a thin line for a moment. Then she continued. " 'And his disciples asked him, saying, Master, who did sin, this man, or his parents, that he was born blind?' "

"Who sinned to make me be blind, Grandma?" asked Fanny.

"Well, dearie, let's wait and see what Jesus said about it. 'Jesus answered, Neither hath this man sinned, nor his parents: but that the works of God should be made manifest in him.' " Grandma stopped. "Theda, can you tell us what Jesus meant there?"

Theda thought for a moment. "There was a reason for the man's blindness," she said. "It was for God's glory."

"Yes," said Grandma. "His blindness was for God's glory."

Fanny heard a familiar step at the door. "Hello, Mama!" she cried.

Grandma looked up as the outside door closed. "Hello, Mercy," she said. "I didn't realize it was so late."

"No, you go on, Mama," said Mercy. "I want to listen." She sat down.

Grandma continued to read. She read about Jesus making clay to put on the man's eyes to heal them, and then telling him to wash.

"Is that what that doctor man tried to do to Fanny?" Polly asked.

"Hush, dear," said Grandma. "Not now."

Grandma continued reading. She read how the man finally found out who had healed him and believed on Jesus. She read about how the Pharisees refused to believe that the man who was healed really was the blind man. Finally she read the last words of the chapter: " 'And Jesus said, For judgment I am come into this world, that they which see not might see; and that they which see might be made blind. And some of the Pharisees which were with him heard these words, and said unto him, Are we blind also? Jesus said unto them, If ye were blind, ye should have no sin: but now ye say, We see; therefore your sin remaineth.' "

Fanny had been listening intently, but now she was confused. "What does that mean, Grandma?" she asked.

"I can tell her, Mama," said Mercy. "Fanny," she said, coming and taking her little daughter into her arms, "it means that there is something far worse than blindness of the eyes. It is blindness of the heart. The Pharisees wouldn't see who Jesus was or why He had come. That means that they were the blindest of all."

5 Waiting for the Postman

It was a Thursday in springtime, and the weather was nice. That meant that Fanny could make her way out to the big rock. There she could wait for the postman to bring the mail.

Fanny loved the soft feel of the dirt and mud under her shoes on the path. When she got to the rock, she walked all the way around it. She felt each of the flowers. "Hello, little daffodils!" she said. "Are you ready for church?"

Fanny climbed on top of the rock and stood up. She held up the tiny book Grandma had let her borrow. Then she lowered her chin to make her voice sound as deep as possible. "Rise!" she commanded the daffodils. "Psalm one hundred twenty-five." Line by line, she recited the psalm, just as the deacon at her church meeting did. She waited after

each line, pretending that her "congregation" was reciting after her.

Then Fanny pretended to be the preacher. Her voice rose and fell, and she waved her arms the way she imagined a preacher must.

After a while, Fanny decided it was time to be a sailor. She knew about sailing from the stories that Grandpa had read. "Row! Row for your lives!" she cried. "Alas, Master Ulysses!"

Now it was time to be a soldier. Fanny had heard many stories about her Pilgrim ancestors. She knew about the many Crosbys and other relatives who had fought in American wars. With her imaginary gun in her hand, Fanny marched alone, tapping her heels on top of that rock. She marched to go fight in the war for independence from England. She marched off to the War of 1812, in which her own Grandpa had fought for real.

Finally Fanny became tired. She sat down on the sunny rock and began one of her favorite activities, singing. "Hail, Columbia, happy land," she sang. "Hail, ye heroes, heaven-born band! Who fought and bled in freedom's cause, And when the storm of war was gone, Enjoyed the peace your valor won!"

After she tired of singing, Fanny just sat. She loved to listen to the sounds of nature. The trees rustled with the new leaves of spring. The daffodils at the foot of the rock whispered to her. Fanny turned her head toward the sound of first one bird, and then another. "I hear you, Mr. Blue Jay," she whispered. "Hello, little Miss Wren."

Then Fanny heard a new kind of rustling. It wasn't the wind this time, but a person's steps. It was the postman, finally come. "Hello, Mr. Reed!" Fanny said.

"Hello, little one," said Mr. Reed. "I have a letter for your family. I hope you haven't been waiting long for me."

"Oh, no," replied Fanny. "Not long at all."

Fanny took the letter politely and carefully walked back to the house. She knew the path so well that it seemed almost as if she could see where she was going. She settled in Grandma's lap for a snuggle while Grandma opened the letter.

Fanny heard her own mother's footsteps at the door. "Hello, Mama!" she cried.

"Hello, my dear," replied Mercy. She kissed her daughter and sat wearily in a chair.

"Was it a hard day, Mercy?" asked Grandma.

"Oh, Mama," sighed Mercy. "I'm used to hard work. It isn't just that . . ." She began to cry again, as she had many evenings over the past five years.

"Now, now, dearie," soothed Grandma. "Not now. We'll talk about it later, after the little ones are in bed."

Late that night, Fanny listened to her mother's soft, muffled sobs. In the tiny house she could hear almost every word. "I never get to see her. . . . I'm so tired when I get home. . . . She's growing up without me. . . . What's going to become of her? . . . No father. . . . Can't see a thing. . . . Will we ever have enough money? . . . How can she learn? . . . It's just too hard. . . . Why isn't God helping us?"

Fanny heard Grandma's soothing voice, as she had many other nights. "There, there, dearie. The Lord knows. We'll just keep calling out to Him. He will hear us, dearie. He's helping us. He can show us the way out of this dark time. We'll just remember that the Master said, 'When thou passest through the waters, I will be with thee.' You know what I like to say, Mercy. 'What can't be cured can be endured.' If He doesn't answer your prayer, that's because He has something even better for you."

Fanny thought about getting out of bed and going to kiss her mama. But she was just too tired. She fell asleep thinking of Grandma's words, "What can't be cured can be endured." She wasn't quite sure what it meant. But she liked the way the words sounded together.

6 Going to the Great City

"Fanny," called Mercy one evening, "come inside, please." Fanny ran in quickly at her mother's call.

Mercy took her five-year-old daughter on her lap. "Fanny, I have something important to say to you," she said. "Tomorrow we are going to go on a trip. It will be a long trip—longer than you've ever been on before. We'll ride in a wagon for a long time. Then we will come to the big river, the Hudson River, and then we'll get on a boat and sail for a long time. Then we'll come to a great city. We'll stay there for several days. And then we will come home again."

Immediately Fanny was filled with questions. "Who is going? Will Grandma and Polly be going?"

"No, dear. It will just be you and me."

"What will we do at the great city?"

"We will visit a famous doctor."

"Where will we stay?"

"With some friends."

"May I please take Temperance with me?" Temperance was Fanny's cornhusk doll.

"Yes, certainly. But you must get to bed now. We have to leave in the morning before it gets light."

Many times Fanny had imagined being on a boat, but she had never actually been on one. And the only city she had ever been to was the village of Doanesburg. There, she knew, was the church, a post office, a library, and a school. She tried to imagine a city being greater than that one. What else could there be?

Early the next morning, Fanny snuggled next to her mother in the wagon. She had a snack of bread and cheese beside her and Temperance in her lap. Softly, under her breath, she sang. But she could tell that her mother felt very stiff beside her.

Finally Fanny asked politely, "Mama, could you please tell me a story?"

"Not now, dear," answered Mercy. "Mama is praying."

Fanny and her mother rode in the wagon almost all day. When they finally arrived at the great river, Fanny needed no more stories. She could feel the wind rushing across the water, against her face. She could hear the lapping of the river waves against the bank. Her eyes could tell that the sun was glinting off the river. And she heard voices—many voices. It was more voices at once than she had ever heard.

"Mama!" Fanny trembled with excitement. "Why are all these people here? Is this a church?"

"No, dear," answered Mama. "The men who are yelling are the sailors. They're getting the boat ready to go down the river. The other people are people like you and me. They are getting on the boat to go to the great city."

Fanny walked carefully with her mother up the boat ramp. A sailor helped them step in. A man with a deep voice greeted them.

"Was that man the captain, Mama?" Fanny asked.

"Yes, dear. How could you tell?"

"Captains always have deep voices," answered Fanny.

Mercy had to laugh at this. "And how many captains have you known?" she asked.

"I know because of the way Grandpa reads the *Odyssey!*" Fanny replied. "Mama, may I please meet the captain?"

"Perhaps. After the boat is underway. He is very busy right now."

Finally the boat was successfully sailing down the river. Then Mercy helped her little girl find the captain.

"Hello, sir!" said Fanny.

"Well, ahoy, there, little miss," replied Captain Greene in his deep voice. "And what brings you to my sloop today?"

"We are going to a great city to see a great doctor!" said Fanny. "We will stay for several days. Then we will come home again."

"Oh, I see," replied the captain. He looked up at Mercy, who placed her hand on Fanny's head. "And have you ever met a ship's captain before?" he asked.

"No, sir! Do you have any sea yarns to tell me?"

The captain laughed a loud, deep laugh. "Yes, I do, probably more than you have time to hear."

"Oh, please tell me!"

"Well, I haven't always sailed a sloop down to the big city and back. I used to go a-sailing on the great sea!"

"Was it the same sea that Odysseus sailed?" Fanny asked.

"No, it was the Atlantic Ocean. For a while I sailed in a whaling ship. We would catch huge whales. They were bigger than this boat, bigger than a huge ship. Sometimes they would come up under the ship and almost turn it over. Sometimes we'd catch one, but he'd start swimming as hard as he could and pull the ship way out to sea! It was a dangerous life. But we did it so we could get the whale oil that you use to light your lamps in your house."

"I know," said Fanny with delight. "I like the lamplight, because I can see it a little bit. Grandma told me that the oil comes from whales."

Every time the boat stopped to pick people up or let people off, the captain had to excuse himself to do his work. But when they were sailing again, he would come back.

"For a while," he told Fanny, "I sailed with a trading ship. We loaded up our ship with lumber and iron and cloth and even hats! Then we would sail down the coast of America. We'd stop and trade with people all the way down. We even sailed all the way to South America. That's where it's warm all year round. We would bring back things like coffee and molasses. One time, little lady, a pirate ship sailed right up to us. They were flying their Jolly Roger—their pirate flag. The captain called to us and told us to turn over all our goods. Well, we had to do it. They were pointing all their guns at us."

The captain talked and talked, but finally he said, "Now, do you have any stories to tell me?"

Fanny thought for a moment. "I don't have any stories as good as yours. But I can sing for you."

"I'd love to hear you sing," said the captain.

Fanny sang one song after another. She sang "Hail Columbia" and "Fourscore and Ten Old Bachelors." The captain laughed till he cried. Several sailors and even some passengers clapped and cheered.

Finally, after many hours the boat landed in the harbor of the great city. It was the city for which their state was named: New York.

7 Visiting the Great Doctor

Fanny had thought the first harbor was busy. But she was overwhelmed by this one. The voices swirled and swarmed around her like the caws of a huge flock of crows. Her mother explained that there were many, many boats here. The boats came here from many places. People were coming and going. As Fanny and her mama climbed down off the sloop, other people were waiting to climb up.

Fanny gripped her mother's hand tightly and couldn't stop trembling. But over the din of people's voices she heard the sound of a new kind of bird.

"Mama, what kind of bird is that?" she asked. "I've never heard it before! It's screaming!"

"They're large and white," Mercy answered. "They land around the people. Some of the people are throwing them scraps of food."

"Sea gulls, they're called, mum!" called a sailor.

"Screaming sea gulls," Fanny murmured. She gripped her mother's hand tighter as they hurried away from the harbor.

Soon Mercy found the friend they were supposed to meet, Mr. Smith. They climbed into his carriage to go to his house. All the way there, Fanny could hardly believe the noise she could hear in this great city. There were sounds of carriages all around and people shouting and horses neighing.

Fanny's mama seemed more cheerful. She talked during almost the whole ride. "There are buildings everywhere, Fanny," she said. "Some of them are very, very tall. They look as tall as two or three of our houses on top of each other. There are many roads crossing each other, not just the road that we're on. All the roads have buildings and people and carriages."

"Why are there so many people, Mama?" Fanny couldn't understand it. "What are they all doing? Why don't they go home?"

"Well, for many of them, like Mr. Smith, this great city *is* their home. Some of them are here to do business, like us. Some of them have just come from the old country to find freedom in our land. Look! I see the dentist's office. He has a picture of a tooth outside his shop."

Fanny felt inside her mouth. "What else do you see?" she asked.

"There's a barber. He has a big picture of scissors outside his shop. And a dry goods store, and a huge stable, and more places than you could imagine, Fanny."

"Oh, my," Fanny breathed.

Finally they were at Mr. Smith's house. Fanny and her mother quickly changed their clothes and fixed their hair. Then it was time to go see the famous doctor.

Down one of those busy streets they traveled again. There was the sign: "Dr. Mott, Eye Specialist." Fanny and her mother climbed up many stairs to get to a dark room. There they sat quietly and waited. Fanny was too frightened to say much.

Finally a kind lady said, "You may see the doctor now." Fanny held her mother's hand as they walked into another little room.

A man came in. "I am Doctor Mott," he said.

"Are you the great doctor?" Fanny asked.

Dr. Mott chuckled. "We'll see about that," he said. "Fanny, I have something for you."

Fanny reached out and felt a little doll. She was not made of cornhusks like Temperance. Instead, she had a china head. Fanny gasped in amazement as she felt the tiny nose and lips and eyes. "Thank you!" she cried.

"Now, Fanny," said the doctor kindly, "I want you to sit very still. I will hold a lamp up to your eyes. I want you to try not to blink."

Fanny sat obediently. She held her eyes open and answered Dr. Mott's questions. The whole time, her fingers kept feeling the beautiful face of the little doll Dr. Mott had given her.

After a while, another doctor came in. He also studied Fanny's eyes for a very long time. He shone lights and asked questions. Fanny finally began to squirm.

Dr. Mott set the lamp down and laid his hand gently on Fanny's head. He talked to Mercy in quiet

tones. "That mustard plaster on your daughter's eyes ruined them."

"Yes, I know," Mercy murmured.

"Her eyes have thick scars on them," the doctor continued. "Looking through her eyes is like looking through frosted glass. She can see light and a little bright color, but nothing else."

Then Dr. Mott leaned over and spoke to Fanny. "Little girl," he said, "would you like me to do something to your eyes that might help you to see a little?"

Fanny pulled back and took hold of her mother's hand. "Would it hurt?" she asked.

"Yes, I'm afraid it would," Dr. Mott replied.

Her voice was barely a whisper. "No, thank you, sir," she said.

The doctor looked up at Mercy and whispered too. "I'm afraid it wouldn't be worth it," he said. "We don't even know if what we could do would help at all. There may even be other damage to the eyes that we don't know about now. I'm afraid she'll never be able to see."

Fanny was startled to hear her mother begin to cry. Quickly a nurse led Fanny outside the door, but she could still hear her mother inside. "I have waited and prayed for five years!" Fanny heard Mercy cry. "I have hoped and saved . . . for . . . five . . . years. But the Lord will not hear my prayer."

For the rest of their time in New York, Fanny tried to comfort her mother. But Mercy just wanted to rest. On the trip back, Fanny had time to herself to sit by the edge of the boat. Her eyes could see the bright pattern of light that the sun made on the water. Here she listened to the lap of the waves against the boat as it made its way back up the river. She sang a quiet little song in time with the waves. She sang about ships and seas, about cities and doctors. She sang about Jesus.

And then they were back. Grandpa was there to meet them and take them on the long wagon trip back to their home in Putnam County. "Oh, Papa," Mercy cried.

"Hello, Grandpa!" said Fanny quietly. "See what the doctor gave me." She held up the doll. Fanny told Grandpa a little about her grand trip to the great city.

When they finally reached home, Fanny was put to bed. As she lay there, she once more heard dear Grandma's voice rising and falling. "The good Lord has something better for her, Mercy," Fanny heard Grandma say. "Just trust Him. Trust Him. He is good."

8 Six Miles Away

Not long after this trip to the big city, Fanny's mother had to take a job as a servant in a different home six whole miles away. Fanny had to go to live with her mother in that home.

But Grandma still found a way to visit her little granddaughter often. Each day that she was due, Fanny would wait on the porch for her. She listened for the familiar carriage wheels. When she heard the carriage, she would bound off the steps to meet Grandma.

"I'm getting bigger, Grandma!" Fanny exclaimed. "My arms reach almost all the way around you now!"

Grandma laughed and reached down to give her little girl a kiss.

"Look at the new toy Mama gave me this time, Grandma! See?" Fanny held up a little "jumping man." She squeezed the sticks that made the man jump and jig. Grandma laughed and took Fanny onto her lap.

"Grandma, the children here talk funny. They say *thee* and *thou* instead of *you.*"

"They are Quakers, Fanny," Grandma said. "They don't talk funny. They just talk differently. Do you get along with them?"

"Well . . . pretty well. They talk about how I'm blind and I can't do some things because I can't see."

Fanny could feel Grandma's body grow stiff. "That isn't true, you know," Grandma said. Then she quickly added, "Have you learned the psalm I gave you to memorize last time I was here?"

"Yes, ma'am, I know the whole thing." Fanny recited Psalm 25 word for word. "Do you have another one for me?"

Grandma read Psalm 32 to Fanny over and over. Finally Fanny was sure she could remember it. "I'll be able to say it for you next time you come," she said.

"I'm sure you will," said Grandma. "I've never seen a child with a memory like yours."

"What is Grandpa reading after supper these days, Grandma?" Fanny asked wistfully.

"He's reading *Pilgrim's Progress* again," Grandma answered.

"Oh," sighed Fanny. "I like that one so much better than the *Odyssey*. I like the exciting part when Christian gets his armor. Then he has to fight Apollyon."

"That's the part Grandpa is coming to tonight," Grandma answered. Then she sighed too.

On Grandma's visits, Fanny often told her stories of her adventures in the village. One day when Fanny was seven, she exclaimed to Grandma, "I climbed higher in the tree than anybody else except Enoch!"

Mercy passed by, on her way to the kitchen with a bucket of hot water. "Enoch is two years older than Fanny," she explained. "And he can see!"

Grandma laughed. "Well," she said, "if Fanny had been able to see, she might not have dared to climb quite so high."

"They told me I couldn't do it because I couldn't see, but I said I would show them. And I did."

"Tell Grandma what else you did last week, that got you into trouble," Fanny's mother said.

"Oh." Fanny blushed. "Well, Grandma, Enoch and some of the other children said I couldn't ride a horse by myself because I couldn't see. I told them I could. So some of the boys helped me climb up on Jack—that's Enoch's father's horse. But Jack didn't have a saddle, so I just hung on to his mane. Jack got scared and started galloping, but I hung on, Grandma! I didn't fall off."

"Oh, goodness, Fanny," Grandma gasped. "You might have gotten hurt. You might have broken your leg!"

"But they were wrong, Grandma! I could do it."

"Yes, dearie. But remember, you want to show good sense too."

One day when Fanny was eight, she sat on the floor next to Grandma's rocking chair. She ran her fingers along the grooves in the old pine boards. Grandma rocked slower and slower. The pine boards creaked more and more quietly. Fanny knew Grandma was waiting patiently to hear whatever it was she wanted to say.

Finally Fanny sighed, "Grandma, they're always telling me that I can't do things because I can't see. I can't climb a tree—but I showed them that I could! I can't ride a horse—but I did that too!" She stopped and sighed again. Finally she said, "But there's one thing I can't do. I can't read. I can't learn the way the other children learn, because I can't go to school. Grandma, more than anything, I want to be able to learn!" Fanny laid her head on Grandma's thin leg and rubbed her weary eyes.

Grandma took Fanny in her arms once again, even though her granddaughter was growing big. For a moment she just rocked. She prayed silently for the right words. Then she spoke. "Fanny, dearie," she said, "listen closely, because this is important. There's nothing greater in this world that we can do than pray. When we pray, we're talking to God Himself. Cry out to Him when you're sad. Nothing is too hard for Him. Your loving Heavenly Father will give you what you ask for if it's good for you. If He doesn't, it's because He has something

better. Whatever your affliction is, you can bear it cheerfully. That's because He's using it to lead you to something even better."

"All right, Grandma," said Fanny. "I will." She wrapped her arms around Grandma's neck and held her face close to Grandma's tight bun of soft brown hair.

That evening, after Grandma was gone, Fanny felt her way to the rocking chair where they had been sitting together earlier. She turned her face toward the window. There she could see the moonlight streaming in. Fanny thought about what Grandma had said. Quietly she knelt and prayed.

The next time Grandma visited, Fanny could hardly wait to tell her news. "Grandma!" she cried. "The other night, after you talked to me, I came here and prayed. I was thinking about the things you said. I felt discouraged, but I really, really talked to my loving Heavenly Father. I did it just the way you said to do. I asked Him if somehow, in all this great world, He had a place for a little blind girl like me. And it seemed as if He spoke to me in my heart. It seemed as if He said, 'Do not be discouraged, little girl. You shall someday be happy and useful, even in your blindness.' So then the next day, I was thinking more about that. And then I thought of a poem. Would you like to hear it?"

"I would like that very much, my dear little girl," said Grandma.

Fanny cleared her throat and shyly began.

"Oh, what a happy child I am,
Although I cannot see!
I am resolved that in this world
Contented I will be!

How many blessings I enjoy
That other people don't!
So weep or sigh because I'm blind,
I cannot—and I won't."

9 Goodbye, Grandma

Once again Fanny and her mother moved. This time it was to Connecticut. It was so far away that Grandma couldn't visit often anymore. During the day Fanny stayed with a Christian lady named Mrs. Hawley.

"What a memory you do have, Fanny Crosby!" Mrs. Hawley exclaimed one day. "As fast as I can read you a chapter of the Bible, you memorize it!"

"I recite the longest verses in Sunday school too." Fanny answered, with a toss of her head. "I'm showing them that a blind girl can do just as well as anyone else . . . and better. I can recite more verses than any of the other students!"

"Well, you must guard against pride," said Mrs. Hawley wisely. "But I do declare, I don't think I've ever seen anyone with a memory like yours. How much of the Bible have you learned now?"

"Let's see," said Fanny. "I know Genesis, Exodus, Leviticus, Numbers, and Deuteronomy. I know all the Gospels, and Ruth, and Song of Solomon, and all of Proverbs, and a lot of the Psalms."

"That will serve you well the rest of your life, young lady," said Mrs. Hawley. "Whenever you want to *read* the Bible, all you'll have to do is think about these Scriptures you've learned."

Mrs. Hawley enjoyed telling Fanny stories. One of her favorites was a story about George Washington when he was a little boy.

"His father had just planted a fine young cherry tree," Mrs. Hawley said. "And young George took that little hatchet he had just been given for his birthday. And he chopped that tree down! Then, when his father found his tree chopped down, he was quite angry. He cried out, 'Who chopped down my cherry tree?' Young George was filled with truthfulness. He marched right up to his father and said, 'I did it, Father, with my little hatchet.' "

"But Mrs. Hawley," Fanny asked, "how could he have been so very honest? He knew he was going to be punished."

"That shows what a fine man he was going to become," answered Mrs. Hawley. "He was filled with truthfulness."

"But . . ." Fanny pondered. "I just wonder. How can anybody be as good as George Washington?"

"He became the Father of his Country, you know," replied Mrs. Hawley.

Later that week Fanny was walking in Mrs. Hawley's garden. The story of George Washington was far from her mind. She felt the soft velvet petals of Mrs. Hawley's prize roses. She knew she shouldn't pluck one, but she did anyway. Then she hid the rose in a secret place.

"Fanny," called Mrs. Hawley later. "Do you know what happened to the rose that was growing right here on this bush?"

Fanny reached up to touch the spot. Then she put her head down. "No, ma'am," she said.

Mrs. Hawley didn't speak for a moment. Then she said, "Fanny, come with me. I have a story I want to read to you."

She took Fanny's hand and led her inside. There she opened the Bible to the book of Acts. "You know the story of Ananias and Sapphira," she said. "They both lied to the Holy Spirit. So the Lord struck them both dead." Mrs. Hawley read the first eleven verses of the fifth chapter of Acts. Then she closed the Bible and left the room.

Fanny sat on the stool. She sighed heavily and twisted her fingers together. Finally she got up and felt her way out of the parlor and into the kitchen. "Mrs. Hawley?" she began. "I . . . I didn't tell the truth before. I picked your rose."

"That's a good girl, Fanny," Mrs. Hawley replied. "I knew you had done it."

"So did the Lord," Fanny sighed.

One day when Fanny was eleven, her mother had some sad news. "Fanny, my dear," she said. "This letter says that Grandma is very sick. We must go to her right away."

Fanny snuggled up to her mother the whole way back to Putnam County. Again and again she asked, "Mama, is Grandma going to be all right?"

"I don't know, my dear," Mama answered. "We must trust the Lord."

It seemed very hard to Fanny to trust the Lord about such a thing.

When they arrived, there was Grandma, sitting in her favorite rocking chair. But something seemed different. She didn't get up. When she spoke, her voice was weak. "Fanny, I won't be with you much longer," she whispered. "Grandma is going home. I'll be in heaven soon."

"No, Grandma!" Fanny cried. She began to sob and threw her arms around Grandma's thin neck.

"Yes, dearie. It's the will of our loving heavenly Father. But Fanny, I have to ask you a question before I go."

"What is it, Grandma?" Fanny managed to say.

"Tell me, my darling, will you meet Grandma in our Father's house on high?"

Fanny couldn't say anything for a moment. She didn't know the answer! She could feel her grandmother's eyes looking at her. But finally she choked out, "By the grace of God, I will."

"Oh, thank the Lord!" Grandma cried. She hugged Fanny close. "Oh, loving Heavenly Father," she prayed. "This may be my last time with my little girl. Look down on us now, dear Lord. Answer my prayer, and bring my little girl safely into Your kingdom some day."

A short time later, Fanny's Grandma died. Her last words to Fanny, "Will you meet Grandma in our Father's house on high?" were words that Fanny never forgot.

10 A Chance to Learn

"Fanny, dear, listen to this."

Fourteen-year-old Fanny could hear the paper rustling as her mama's hand trembled.

"It says, 'The New York Institution for the Blind was founded in 1831 with only three students. Now generous people around the state are helping us. Now we are able to teach thirty students without charge. We hope for many more. We want all people to understand that, with the right teaching, the blind can learn as well as others.' " Mama's voice shook on the last few words.

Fanny gasped. "Oh, thank God!" she cried. "Thank God! He has answered my prayer! I knew He could. Mama, where is the school?"

"It's in Manhattan. In New York City. That's a long way."

"I know. I remember from when we went when I was little. But Mama, if I go there, I can finally learn—literature and music and writing and history and philosophy. I could truly learn. I know I can be a good student. I know I can! Oh, Mama, this is the happiest day of my life!"

Fanny and her mother prepared for Fanny to leave on the long trip to go to live at the school for the blind. The morning she was to leave, Fanny's teeth chattered—not from cold, but from fear. This would be her first time away from her family. "Mama, I c-can't do my b-buttons," she stammered. "Please help me." Mama patiently did Fanny's twenty-eight buttons. She blinked back her own tears while she did it.

Fanny pushed away the oatmeal her mother had prepared. "I—I can't eat it, Mama. I have a big lump in my throat. It won't go down."

"Take some bread and cheese with you, then," said Mama. "It's a long trip." Then she took her daughter by the shoulders. "Fanny," she said, "I will miss you."

Fanny gulped back a sob.

"And you will miss me," Mama continued. "But remember, this is God's answer to your prayer.

You're going to get to learn. You'll learn things that I would never be able to teach you."

"Yes, Mama," gulped Fanny. She threw her arms around her mama one last time and then picked up her bag and hurried out the door. She refused to turn around again, fearful that she would run back. She reached out for the arm of the lady who was going with her in the stagecoach to the coast where they would take a steamboat to Manhattan.

There were no highways and bridges for the stagecoach to travel over. There were only rough roads and boats. This sixty-mile trip took four days.

In the stagecoach, Fanny sat next to her friend, trembling and shaking. Finally the lady said, "Fanny, should we go back?"

Fanny thought and thought for a long time. Should she go back? If she went on, she would miss her mother, she knew. But how much she longed to learn! Could she be happy in the village, growing up with no real education? Wouldn't she just be frustrated for the rest of her life?

"No," she said finally. "I will go on." She turned her face toward the window of the stagecoach.

There she could feel the rising sun shining on her eyes.

After four days of traveling, Fanny arrived in Manhattan at the New York Institution for the Blind. The school was a mile or so from the coast, out in the country. Fanny was thankful for this. She could hear the same bird songs that she had heard back home in Putnam County.

Fanny held on to her friend's arm. Together they walked up the unfamiliar steps and into the large room. A lady immediately came up to them. "Is thee our new student?" she asked gently.

"Yes, ma'am. Frances Jane Crosby," said Fanny. She trembled a little.

"Well, Frances, we want thee to be at home here. I'll be glad to help thee find everything thee needs."

"Thee is a Quaker, ma'am?" Fanny's face brightened a little. "I knew some Quakers in North Salem."

"I have cousins in North Salem," answered the lady. "It is a good place."

FANNY CROSBY: QUEEN OF GOSPEL SONGS

Fanny said goodbye to her friend. Then she clutched her bag tightly as she took the arm of this kind lady. How strange the clacking of her shoes sounded in the unfamiliar hallway!

The kind lady led Fanny to a little room. "This will be thy room, Fanny," she said. "Here is thy bed."

Fanny felt carefully for the bed and sat down. She still clutched the bag that held all her things. How strange everything seemed! How different it all was from home! Fanny didn't want the tears to start coming. But they did, anyway, just a little.

"Oh, Fanny, dear," asked the lady, "is this thy first time away from home?"

"Yes, ma'am," Fanny barely managed to say. She thought about the mother she had left behind and wouldn't see again for a very long time. Then she gasped, "Excuse me, ma'am, but I have to cry!" And she began to wail loudly. Out came all the tears she had wanted to cry during the long, long trip.

11 The Poetess of the Institution

Time passed, and Fanny began to learn her way around the school. In fact, she began to think of the Institution as her home, but she struggled with some of her studies.

"I simply cannot learn division!" Fanny cried out one day. Tears of frustration came into her eyes.

Fanny's friend Anna patted her arm. "I know it's hard for you," she said. "You just have to keep working at it."

"I just can't," Fanny sighed. "I absolutely *love* English and history and astronomy. And I *adore* music class. But math . . . I should write a 'poem of frustration' about it." Then she added, "And I ought to write a poem about Braille. I just cannot read those little dots with my fingers! I do much better when the teachers read the books out loud to us."

"I'm sure it would be a funny poem, if you did write one," said Anna. "You made the whole group laugh after supper the other night when you said,

> 'Now just as sure as I'm a sinner,
>
> I know I've had a very good dinner!' "

"Yes, and I laughed the hardest of all," chuckled Fanny. "I mean to be a very famous poetess one day. I'm going to show them that a blind person can do just as well as a seeing person."

Fanny became popular at the school. She could play several instruments, sing, and make funny jokes. Most of all, she could think up poetry from morning till night. She even wrote several poems for the Institution in honor of special people or special occasions. Fanny began to be well known not just in the school, but in the whole city!

One day Fanny was called into the office of Dr. Jones, the school superintendent. "You sent for me, sir?" she asked. She wondered what kind of poetry she was going to be asked to write this time.

"Yes, I did, Miss Crosby," Dr. Jones answered. "I have been told that our young poetess is becoming very proud of her accomplishments."

Fanny didn't know what to say. "I . . . uh . . . well . . ." she faltered.

"Miss Crosby," he continued, "do not depend on the praise of men. Think more about what you can become rather than what people will think of you."

Fanny was speechless. Dr. Jones continued. "Remember that whatever talents you have belong to God. You ought to give Him the credit for all that you do."

Fanny felt the tears stinging her eyes. For a moment she sat still. But then, suddenly, she practically jumped out of her chair. She came around the desk to hug the surprised Dr. Jones. "Thank you for saying that, Dr. Jones!" she cried. "You spoke to me as my father would have if he had been living. I will remember your words."

It wasn't long before Dr. Jones called Fanny into his office again. "Miss Crosby," he said, "I believe you are spending too much time on your rhymes.

You are not spending enough time on your studies. Because of that, you may not write any poetry for three months."

"No poetry—" Fanny took a gasping breath. She couldn't believe it. "But poetry constantly comes into my mind!" she said. "How can I keep that from happening?"

"You can't stop it from coming into your mind," Dr. Jones answered. "But you can keep yourself from thinking about it. You can refuse to say it out loud."

It was a very sad young lady who left Dr. Jones's office that morning. As the days went by, Fanny became more and more discouraged. She could hardly eat or sleep. Her studies didn't improve. Instead, they failed miserably.

"What is the matter with you, Miss Crosby?" Dr. Jones finally asked her. "Why are you doing such poor work lately?"

"Oh, Dr. Jones," Fanny replied, "I just can't do anything, really. Poetry fills my mind. But you have told me that I can't say any of it or even think about it. I'm so miserable! I can't think about anything else."

Dr. Jones had to chuckle. "Very well, Miss Crosby," he replied. "Just pay more attention in your classes. You can think about your poetry."

From that time on, Fanny became one of the best students in the school. Her poetry became more and more well known. Important people began to visit the blind school just so they could meet Fanny Crosby.

In the summer of 1842, Fanny traveled with some of the other students to other parts of New York state. When she got back, she asked a friend to help her with a letter to her mother.

August 1842

Mother Dear,

I've just returned from our big trip up the Hudson River and along the Erie Canal. What a time we had! Twenty students and three teachers all traveling together by boat! But it was a time I shall never forget.

At every town we stopped to put on our presentation to raise money for the Institution. I played the harp and the piano for them. We sang together, and I sang solos. I also recited poetry, of course, just as I do back at school.

I think a lot of the people who came to see us were there just because they were curious. They didn't think blind people could do anything, you know! Every place we stopped, the people were amazed. Many people gave money, so our trip was a success.

Mother, you wouldn't believe some of the funny questions people ask! One that I hear most often is, "When you eat, how do you get the food to your mouth?" It seemed like such a silly question that I thought up a silly answer. Now I tell people, "I tie one end of a string to the table leg. I tie the other end to my tongue. Then I work the food up along the string until it finally gets to my mouth." Some of the people aren't sure whether to believe me or not!

Oh, Mother dear, I can never thank you enough for sending me to the Institution. It's hard for both of us to be separated from one another, but this is the place where I belong.

Your loving daughter,
Fanny

12 Family Ties

While Fanny was away at school, she received some happy news. Her mother had married again! Later two little half-sisters were born, named Julia and Carrie. Fanny was twenty when Julia was born.

Every summer Fanny went to visit her family. The two little girls would gaze in awe at their famous grown-up sister.

One evening in the summer of 1848, the family sat around the supper table. Mama asked, "What important people have you met since your last visit, Fanny?"

Fanny laughed. "Well, President Polk came to visit again last month. This time he came without telling us ahead of time. I had already met him, you know, so I was the one chosen to walk with him. He's been sick, and he just wanted a quiet visit. We didn't have a big assembly the way we did when President Tyler came unannounced."

"What happened when President Tyler came?" Julia asked.

"Why, didn't I ever tell you about that?" Fanny answered her eight-year-old sister. "That was a few years ago. As I said, we didn't know he was coming. Just suddenly, there he was. He came with the mayor and all the city councilmen! You should have seen the superintendent, Julia. He came running in to me and said, 'Miss Crosby, Miss Crosby, the President is here. The President *of the United States!*' Then he gasped, 'We'll have a special assembly for him in fifteen minutes. Of course we need a poetic greeting. Can you write one and recite it for us at the assembly?' So I did."

"In fifteen minutes?" Julia gasped.

"Yes," said Fanny. She smiled and took a bite of her potato.

"So how many presidents have you met now, Fanny?" Mercy asked. Fanny could feel the satisfaction in her mother's voice.

"Let's see," said Fanny. She put her fork down to count on her fingers. "There was President Tyler, as I said. There was President Polk last month, and twice before that. Then, you know, I talked with President Adams when I spoke before Congress four years ago. He wasn't president anymore, but just a congressman by then. Does that still count?"

"Yes, that counts!" said Julia. "And didn't you go out to dinner with one?"

"Oh, yes, you must have been reading some of my old letters, Julia!" Fanny teased. "President Van Buren. He was one of the most charming presidents I've ever met. And I've been out to dinner with him more than once!"

"Did you write any poems for him?"

"Of course!" answered Fanny. "And for the others too. Would you like to hear some of them?"

"Yes, yes!" cried Julia and Carrie. "Come in here!" They pulled Fanny into the parlor, where they argued over whose turn it was to sit in her lap. Mercy sat and beamed with joy over her famous daughter.

Fanny recited poetry to her little sisters all evening. One of them was the poem she wrote for President Tyler. The last two lines said,

"And this the glad song of our nation shall be:
Hurrah for John Tyler and liberty's tree!"

"More, more," cried the little sisters, clapping. "That was so beautiful!"

"You must be the greatest poet in all of history," Julia sighed.

"I don't think I'll ever be that," Fanny laughed. "But I'm glad I'm the greatest to *you*."

After the little ones were in bed, Fanny sat with her mother. For a while they both rocked quietly in their rocking chairs. "Your Grandma was right, Fanny," said Mercy. "The Lord didn't give you sight, but He gave you something better. You have a great talent."

"Yes, Mother, and other things too. I've been able to really learn there at the school. I even get to teach now. And I meet famous and exciting people. I have a good life."

They rocked in silence for a few more minutes. Then Mercy asked quietly, "Is the Lord Jesus in your life, Fanny?"

Fanny laughed quickly, feeling embarrassed. "He's in my life . . . in a way," she answered. "I still sometimes think about the things you and Grandma taught me. But I'm so busy, Mother! So busy, and so happy. The people love me there. Those childhood days seem like a long, long time ago."

13 Death and Life

One afternoon, in the summer of 1849, the superintendent rushed into Fanny's office at the school. "Miss Crosby!" he cried frantically, "will you promise not to tell what has happened?"

"Why, yes, Mr. Chamberlain!" Fanny replied. "Whatever is wrong?"

"A man—here in the city—has come down with . . . with the disease!"

"The disease? You mean cholera?"

"Yes, the epidemic has come here! He died on the way to the hospital. It can't be long before the students here at the school will be struck with it."

"You're right," said Fanny grimly. "Once one person gets it, it will spread all over the city."

It wasn't long. In a few days one of the little girls was sick. "Miss Crosby, please come here," she whispered weakly. "Please take me on your lap."

Fanny pulled the little girl to her. "I am going home, Miss Crosby. I just want to say goodbye and tell you that I love you." Fanny held the dying girl and sobbed.

The days passed. Almost all the schoolchildren had been sent home until the cholera epidemic was over. Fanny decided to ask if she could help at the hospital.

The nurse at the hospital looked at Fanny. "But . . . you're blind," she said. "How can you help?"

Fanny pulled back at the harsh sound of the woman's voice, but she answered bravely. "I can be a great help," she said. "I can mix cholera medicine and fluff people's pillows and . . . and hold sick children when they're dying. . . ." Her voice caught in her throat.

"Well, we do need the help," sighed the nurse. "Do what you can."

Fanny walked down the hall behind the nurse's rustling skirt. From every room she could hear the moans of people. "Do many of the people who come here die?" she asked the nurse.

"Yes," the nurse replied quickly. "Very many."

Day after day Fanny helped at the hospital the best she could. More and more people filled the rooms. Fanny stumbled over the beds to move about as she tried to give one person a sip of water or put a cool cloth on another person's head. Fanny found that many children from the blind school had come. As she held each child, she remembered her grandma's words from long ago. "Trust the good Lord above," she told the children. "He will not leave us. He will do whatever is best for us."

The halls were crowded too. Every day coffins piled up in the hallway—large and small—as one person died after another.

One evening Fanny asked one of the doctors, "How many people have died in the city this week?"

"Five hundred," he replied. "Five hundred every week. Former President Polk died last night."

Fanny set her mouth grimly. "I would like to write a poem to honor him," she said. "But I have too many dying all around me."

Early every morning, a man with a huge old wagon came clattering down the street. "Bring out your dead!" his harsh voice cried. Fanny stood back as the coffins were carried out from the hospital. She sensed that people were carrying out coffins from all the houses around. She heard them pile the wooden boxes on the wagon. Then the wagon master clattered down the street that led outside the city. There, she knew, he would bury them all in a huge grave. Morning after weary morning came the cry, "Bring out your dead!"

After the cholera epidemic ended, Fanny sank into a deep sadness. For months she couldn't seem to be able to come out of it.

But all that changed one autumn evening.

November 21, 1850

Mother Dear,

I haven't written in quite a while, I know. But I have to tell you about what happened last night.

The cholera epidemic was like a terrible nightmare. I kept being afraid that I would get the disease and die. I kept thinking about what Grandma said the night before she died. "Will you meet Grandma in our Father's house on high?" But I didn't know the answer.

Then one night I dreamed that a dear friend here was dying too. In my dream, he asked me the same question. But I wasn't sure if I would meet any of the people of God in that fair land above!

Then Mr. Camp invited me to go to the revival meetings at his church. At first I didn't want to, but finally I went. Last night I walked to the front of the church to pray. I listened to the people sing.

Alas! and did my Saviour bleed?
And did my Sovereign die?
Would He devote that sacred head
For such a worm as I?

I thought about all that Jesus had done for me. I knew He had died to pay for my sins. I thought about how I didn't deserve to be forgiven, but He wanted to forgive me anyway. Then I heard the people singing the last verse.

But drops of grief can ne'er repay
The debt of love I owe;

Here, Lord, I give myself away—
'Tis all that I can do.

That was it! I knew it! I whispered, "Lord, I
give myself away!" And suddenly I felt my soul
filled with heavenly light. I knew that I had been
trying to hold the world in one hand and the
Lord in the other.

I knew, Mother dear, that you would want to
know my wonderful news. I have entered on a
new life. Your prayers, and Grandma's prayers,
have been answered.

Your loving daughter,

Fanny

14 "The Happiest Creature in All the World!"

Fanny continued to teach at the blind school. She still wrote poetry for all occasions. But now she was a Christian. All the Scriptures she had memorized as a child began to come alive to her. She loved thinking about her Lord Jesus.

When Fanny was thirty-eight years old, she married another blind teacher at the school. His name was Alexander Van Alstyne, and he was also a Christian. Fanny and Van had a little baby, but the baby died while it was still young. Fanny was very sad for a long time. She cried out to the Lord to help her.

The Lord did help her, in a most unusual way. One day in February, 1864, Fanny came into the tiny apartment she shared with her husband. "Van?" she called.

"Yes, Fanny, I'm here," her husband answered.

"Oh, Van! I just got back from Mr. Bradbury's office. He liked the hymn I wrote—he really liked it! He's planning to publish it in his new hymnbook!"

"Fanny, I'm so glad to hear that." Van felt his way to his wife and took her hand.

"Van, I can tell that this is the work God has called me to do. I can feel it! And now, with the great revival in the church, they want new songs. They're publishing many, many new hymnbooks. They want songs about the love of Christ and His great salvation. And His protection, and our desire to live for Him, and our love and praise for Him. Van, I feel a hundred hymns in my head! The Lord has given me a purpose for my life. I'm the happiest creature in all the world!"

"The Lord has brought you out of darkness," said Van.

"Yes," agreed Fanny, "into His marvelous light."

Fanny began to write hymns, sometimes several in a week. More and more music writers called on her to ask her to write words for their tunes. People began to sing her hymns in churches all over the country.

One day Fanny's friend Mr. Doane came to visit. "Fanny," he said, "you've done such a wonderful job writing beautiful hymns. I have a tune here that I would like to be used for a song. Can you write some words for it?" Then he added, "I have only forty minutes before I have to leave on a train. Can you learn the tune and write something while I'm gone?"

Mr. Doane hummed the tune. Fanny listened intently. Then she clapped her hands together and cried, "Why, that tune says, 'Safe in the arms of Jesus!' If you give me a few minutes, I'll see what I can do." She went into another room. There she knelt down to ask the Lord for help. Then she sat and thought and thought, moving her lips, tilting her head. When she came back, she said, "Mr. Doane, how much time do you have left?"

"About ten minutes," he answered.

"Oh, good. That's just enough time for you to write down the hymn!"

"You have finished it?" Mr. Doane could hardly believe his ears.

"Yes, the blessed Holy Spirit gave me the words. I have three verses to dictate to you." And Fanny recited them.

> Safe in the arms of Jesus,
> Safe on His gentle breast,
> There by His love o'ershaded,
> Sweetly my soul shall rest.
>
> Hark! 'tis the voice of angels,
> Borne in a song to me.
> Over the fields of glory,
> Over the jasper sea.
>
> Safe in the arms of Jesus,
> Safe on His gentle breast,
> There by His love o'ershaded,
> Sweetly my soul shall rest.

Mr. Doane loved the hymn. He began using it right away in his Sunday school, and soon it was published in a hymnbook. It became one of the favorite hymns in the country.

Another friend invited Fanny to her house one day. "Fanny, I've written a tune that I want you to listen to," she said. She played the tune, and Fanny listened carefully. Then, as she did whenever she was happy, she clapped her hands together. "That is a beautiful tune!" she said. "And it says, 'Blessed Assurance'!" Quickly she prayed for help from the Lord. Then she thought through the words and asked her friend to write them down.

> Blessed assurance, Jesus is mine!
> Oh, what a foretaste of glory divine!
> Heir of salvation, purchase of God,
> Born of His spirit, washed in His blood.
>
> This is my story, this is my song,
> Praising my Saviour all the day long;
> This is my story, this is my song,
> Praising my Saviour all the day long.

For the next forty years Fanny wrote over two hundred songs each year. Every new hymnbook contained more and more Fanny Crosby songs. In all, she wrote over *eight thousand* hymns.

15 The Queen of Gospel Songs

May, 1886

Mother Dear,

I am so sorry that I cannot be with you on your 85th birthday. I have still been very busy traveling and speaking all over the state and in other states too. These dear people mean so much to me. What a joy it is that the Lord is using my songs to bring them to Christ!

I enjoy my work at the rescue mission more than I can say. Many of the men who have come to Christ have promised never again to drink a drop of strong drink. I know that this will go a long way in keeping them out of trouble. I call the men "my boys"—they mean so much to me.

Perhaps you heard that at President Grant's funeral the song that was played was "Safe in the Arms of Jesus." That might be my favorite of all the songs I've written. I've been able to use it to comfort many sad mothers and fathers whose children have died. Did I tell you that Mr. Sankey even heard some German people singing it when he was visiting in their country?

Mr. Sankey is still singing many of my hymns when Mr. Moody preaches. So many people say that they first understood the gospel when they heard Mr. Moody preach it. Some of them even say that they first understood the gospel when they heard Mr. Sankey sing it! What I want the most from my hymns is for people to be pointed to the dear Lord Jesus.

I still receive callers almost every week, when I'm home. I think they're curious to see an old blind lady! But they come with problems and cares. They need this old blind lady to offer what help I can. I'm so glad I can pray with them and point them to Jesus.

Happy birthday, Mother dear!

We think how devoted our mother's love,
What a sunshine of joy she gives!
And we feel as we tenderly kiss her cheek,
What a comfort that still she lives.

Your loving daughter,

Fanny

As time passed, Fanny was called on to speak more and more often at churches and meeting houses around the country. After Van died, Fanny went to live with her sister in Connecticut. But even there, she also received more and more visitors.

In the winter of 1908 a young reporter knocked on the door of Fanny's house. Fanny's sister Carrie answered the door.

"I'm here to see Mrs. Van Alstyne," said the reporter.

A tiny, stooped old lady entered the parlor. She touched the shelf and the table, stepping quickly. Only her small dark glasses told the reporter that she was blind. "Here I am, young man!" she called. "And you can call me Aunt Fanny. Now that I'm eighty-eight years old, everyone calls me that."

"Just remember, sister," said Carrie, "you have another appointment in an hour."

"I won't forget, Carrie," said Aunt Fanny. "Come into the parlor, my boy, and have a seat. I'm so happy to be able to help you any way I can."

The reporter cleared his throat. "Aunt Fanny," he said, "you're probably the most famous songwriter alive."

Aunt Fanny chuckled. "God bless your dear heart," she said. "I am shut out of the world and shut in with my Lord. The Lord is the sunshine of my soul. To God be the glory!"

"To God be the glory. Is that your favorite of all the hymns you've written?"

Aunt Fanny raised her eyebrows and thought for a moment. "Perhaps," she said. "My favorite changes from time to time, you know." She tapped her wrinkled cheek. "But here is one that is very dear to me." She raised her skinny finger to the sky and in a high, clear voice, recited,

"Rescue the perishing, Care for the dying,
Snatch them in pity from sin and the grave;
Weep o'er the erring one, lift up the fallen,
Tell them of Jesus, the mighty to save.

Rescue the perishing, Care for the dying,
Jesus is merciful, Jesus will save.

"You know, young man," Aunt Fanny said, "there is a story that goes with that song. Years and years ago—forty years, it was—I was speaking at a rescue mission. In my heart I could tell that some mother's boy had gone astray. I said to those men, 'If there is some young man here tonight who has wandered from his mother's home and teaching, would he please come to me after the service?' And sure enough, a young man did come forward. He was saved that night. When I arrived home that evening, I wrote that song.

"And now listen to this." Aunt Fanny clapped her thin hands in delight. "Just recently, I told that story at a meeting. Afterward a man came up to me. He said, 'I was that young man who came to the Lord that night! The Lord truly saved me. And I have tried to be a good Christian ever since.' Oh, my boy, there are many, many stories of these songs being used of the Lord." She picked up the cup of tea Carrie had brought her and took a sip.

"What's the secret?" asked the reporter. "How is it that your songs are so popular and so powerful? And you've written so many!"

"God bless your dear heart, my boy." Aunt Fanny chuckled. "The Lord gives me the words. I still often have to work over them, sometimes for several days. But I always pray before thinking up even one word. That's the reason the songs are used of the Lord to bring so many people to Himself. The blessed Holy Spirit gives me the words. My dear Lord is the delight of my life."

"But how can you be so happy when you're blind? Isn't it hard to forgive the doctor who injured your eyes?"

Aunt Fanny leaned forward and shook her finger in the young man's face. "What good does it do to hold a grudge against anyone?" she asked. "No good at all! No, I have no hard feelings against that man. My grandmother rocked me in her chair and taught me that God would give me what is best for me. And so He has! The Lord has used my blindness to show what He can do. He is the mighty One!"

"Forgiveness and trust. Do you think they are part of your secret of how you've lived so long and stayed so healthy?"

"That's it! Yes, that's it!" Aunt Fanny clapped her hands together again. "Two of my secrets of staying happy and healthy are to control my tongue and to control my thoughts. I never want to say an unkind word. I never want to think an unkind thought. The light of the Lord shines in my soul! If you find anyone happier than I am, I want you to show him to me. My cup of happiness is full to overflowing."

Afterword

"And I Shall See Him Face to Face"

Aunt Fanny loved to write hymns about heaven. One of the best-loved was called "Saved by Grace."

> Some day the silver cord will break,
> And I no more as now shall sing;
> But oh, the joy when I shall wake
> Within the palace of the King!
>
> And I shall see Him face to face,
> And tell the story—Saved by grace;
> And I shall see Him face to face,
> And tell the story—Saved by grace.

This song spread all around the world. It was sung in many languages. When Aunt Fanny's friend, the singer Ira Sankey, died, the chorus of this song were the last words he spoke.

In 1910, Aunt Fanny was ninety years old. Almost all of her friends had died. Even her friends' children had grown old, and many of them had also died. When people first saw Aunt Fanny, they thought she might die soon too. Her skinny face and hands were covered with wrinkles. Her body bent over so much that she could hardly walk. But as soon as she spoke, Aunt Fanny suddenly seemed younger. Her voice sounded clear and high instead of cracked and shaking. People loved to listen to her wonderful stories of the love of God.

One day Aunt Fanny was riding in a coach with a pastor friend. The driver knew that a very old blind lady was his passenger. But then she began to talk with the pastor. "My, how young she sounds," the driver thought. He began to listen as she talked about Jesus.

Finally the driver felt a tap on his arm and heard the pastor say, "This is Fanny Crosby, the hymn writer."

"Fanny Crosby!" the driver cried. He stopped the horse. Then he climbed down from the coach, took off his hat, and opened the coach door. Tears streamed down his face as he looked at the old lady with the small green glasses. "Miss Crosby," he said, "I never thought I'd get to meet you, but I want you to know how much your hymns have meant to me. Ever since my father stopped drinking and came to Jesus, he's been singing your hymns."

Aunt Fanny put her old, wrinkled hand tenderly on the man's arm. "My dear boy," she said, "I thank the dear Lord Jesus for what you just told me."

When they arrived at the train station, the coach driver found a policeman. "This is Miss Fanny Crosby," he said. "Help her and her friend get safely to the train."

The policeman's eyes opened wide. "Fanny Crosby?" he said. "You wrote 'Safe in the Arms of Jesus.' "

"Yes, I did, many years ago," replied Aunt Fanny.

The policeman's eyes began to fill with tears. "We sang that song last week," he said. "We sang it at . . . at . . . my little girl's funeral."

Aunt Fanny took hold of the policeman's arm and felt his tears drop on her hands. "Oh, my dear boy," her gentle voice said quietly, "God bless your dear heart. Please tell your dear wife that your little girl really *is* safe in the arms of Jesus. I shall be praying for you as I go on my way."

Aunt Fanny felt her small, wrinkled hand being grasped in the policeman's big, rough one.

"Thank you," he said.

On she went to tell that story, and many others, to crowds of people. Sometimes five thousand people at a time would gather to hear her speak.

Finally, though, came the time when Aunt Fanny's body began to slow down too. Now she was often just too tired to receive visitors.

Shortly before she died, Aunt Fanny spoke at a little church near her home. The building was filled with violets and packed with people.

"My dear, dear people, I love you dearly," Aunt Fanny said in her high, clear voice. "I want all of you to go to God in prayer in all your trials and sorrows. He will answer your prayers better than you think." She ended by saying, "I believe God still has work for me to do. I don't want to die yet."

But Aunt Fanny's body was wearing out. In February, 1915, just before she turned ninety-five, Aunt Fanny went to sleep for the last time. Then, when she awoke, she found herself "within the palace of the King."

Aunt Fanny had asked that no money be spent on a fancy marble marker for her grave. "I have only done what I can," she had said. "If people want to give something when I die, give money to help poor people." So the only marker on Aunt Fanny's grave was a very small one that said, "Aunt Fanny. She hath done what she could."

The town where Aunt Fanny lived held its largest funeral ever. People lined up for blocks. They wanted to be able to pass by her casket and see "Aunt Fanny" one last time. In a church building full of flowers, the choir sang "Safe in the Arms of Jesus" and "Saved by Grace."

When Fanny Crosby died, she could see at last, for the first time since she was a tiny baby. The first face she saw was the face of her Redeemer, her dear Lord Jesus Christ. He was the one she had lived to serve. He was the one who had made her "the happiest creature in all the world."